Ho'oponopono

Traditional Ways of Healing to Make Things Right Again

Malcolm Nāea Chun

Ka Wana Series

Curriculum Research & Development Group
University of Hawai'i

ISBN 1-58351-042-7
ISBN 1-58351-040-0 (set)

Pihana Nā Mamo: The Native Hawaiian Special Education Project (Grant
Number: H221A000002) is funded by the U.S. Department of Education,
under the Native Hawaiian Education Program as authorized under Part
B of TitleVII of the Elementary and Secondary Education Act of 1965
(ESEA), as amended by the No Child Left Behind Act of 2001 (P.L. 107-
110), and is administered by the Office of Special Education Programs, Office
of Elementary and Secondary Education, U.S. Department of Education.
Opinions expressed herein are those of the author and do not necessarily reflect
the position of the U.S. Department of Education, and such endorsement
should not be inferred.

Series note: Ka Wana Series, Book 5

Book design and layout by Erin Sakihara and Wayne Shishido
Cover design by Robin M. Clark

Distributed by the Curriculum Research & Development Group
University of Hawai'i
1776 University Avenue
Honolulu, HI 96822-2463

E-mail: crdg@hawaii.edu
Web: www.hawaii.edu/crdg

CRDG Pihana Nā Mamo Staff
Morris K. Lai, Principal Investigator
Hugh H. Dunn, Pihana Nā Mamo Director
Malcolm N. Chun, Cultural Specialist
Robin M. Clark, Graphic Artist
Terry Ann F. Higa, Internal Evaluator
Lillian M. Kido, Support Specialist
Mark C. Yap, Media Specialist

Hawai'i Department of Education Pihana Nā Mamo Staff
Gloria S. Kishi, Pihana Nā Mamo Director
Cynthia L. H. Choy, Makua Hānai Coordinator
JoAnn Kaakua, Kāko'o Coordinator
Maggie Hanohano, Heluhelu Coordinator
Doreen K. Yamashiro, Data Coordinator

CRDG Production Staff
Lori Ward, Managing Editor
Lehua Ledbetter, Copyrights
Erin Sakihara, Book design and layout
Robin M. Clark, Cover design

CRDG Administration
Donald B. Young, Director
Kathleen F. Berg, Associate Director

Ka Wana Series

Pono
The Way of Living

Welina
Traditional and Contemporary Ways of Welcome and Hospitality

Aʻo
Educational Traditions

Ola
Traditional Concepts of Health and Healing

Hoʻoponopono
Traditional Ways of Healing to Make Things Right Again

Hoʻomana
Understanding the Sacred and Spiritual

Alakaʻi
Traditional Leadership

Kākāʻōlelo
Traditions of Oratory and Speech Making

Hoʻonohonoho
Traditional Ways of Cultural Management

Kapu
Gender Roles in Traditional Society

Hewa
The Wrong Way of Living

Ka 'Ōlelo Mua
Foreword

The growing need for reconciliation in contemporary society has rekindled an interest in the Native Hawaiian practice of ho'oponopono. Perhaps more than ever, people are in need of new and creative ways to build and strengthen relationships with others.

Ho'oponopono, Traditional Ways of Healing to Make Things Right Again was designed to provide insight and guidance in our understanding of a Hawaiian way of healing and reconciliation. Malcolm Nāea Chun, a cultural specialist with the University of Hawai'i's Curriculum Research & Development Group (CRDG), has researched historical accounts of peace making in Hawai'i and explored modern-day applications of ho'oponopono. For many students and their families, ho'oponopono represents a compelling means by which to restore and mend broken relationships.

This book is part of the Ka Wana Series, a set of publications developed through Pihana Nā Mamo and designed to assist parents, teachers, students, and staff in their study and modern-day application of Hawaiian customs and traditions.

Pihana Nā Mamo is a joint project of CRDG and the Hawai'i Department of Education, and production of the Ka Wana series represents the work of many collaborators. Mahalo to Linda Thomas and Gene Uno for their reading and comments; Lori Ward for her editing and proofreading; Allen Emura and his staff of the DOE Reprographic Section; Puanani Wilhelm and the Hawaiian Studies and Language Section for proofreading the documents; Project Co-Directors Gloria S. Kishi and Hugh

Dunn; the Pihana Nā Mamo ʻohana of the Hawaiʻi Department of Education and the Curriculum Research & Development Group, College of Education, University of Hawaiʻi at Mānoa, and the U.S. Department of Education, which provided the funding for Pihana Nā Mamo.

Morris K. Lai, Principal Investigator
Pihana Nā Mamo

Ōlelo Ha'i Mua
Preface

> Do you believe I'm wearing a kukui lei?
> It's Hawaiian in looks—it's plastic made in Hong Kong.
> That's what became of a lot our beliefs.
> I wore this on purpose. I wanted you to know this is kukui nut.
> It's not kukui nut, but it's Hawaiian, but it's Hawaiian made in
> Hong Kong of plastic, and that's the way a lot of our beliefs
> and customs have become.
> —attributed to Mary Kawena Pukui

Cultural revival and identification have gone beyond academic and intellectual arguments to a reality in communities and families, and are now part of the political landscape of the islands. In asking the question "Who are we?" people are really asking how they see the world differently from others, and how this affects the way they make decisions. These are questions about a people's world view—how they see the world around them, and ultimately, how they see themselves.

In the 1960s, social workers at the Queen Lili`uokalani Children's Center, a trust created to benefit orphaned and destitute Native Hawaiian children, began to notice behaviors of their children and families that were quite different from the textbook cases they had studied in school. In response, the center initiated a project to identify Hawaiian cultural and social practices and behaviors, and to study them as they contrasted with their Western counterparts. The impact and influence of the resulting books, entitled *Nānā I Ke Kumu*, are still felt in Native Hawaiian communities, where the books are now a standard reference.

By 1992 *Nānā I Ke Kumu* was considered historical information, and as the cultural specialist for the Queen Lili`uokalani Children's Center, I became involved in a project to update it. We were still seeing cases that involved Hawaiian cultural practices and behaviors foreign to both Hawaiian and non-Hawaiian workers that needed to be considered in any programs designed to help. We were having to re-adapt traditional healing practices like ho`oponopono to accommodate changes such as family schedules, misunderstanding or not knowing Hawaiian language and concepts, and having non-Hawaiian family members. We realized that there was, once again, a great need for a series that would examine, in depth, key concepts and values for Native Hawaiians to understand and practice today.

This series is intended to fill that need. Each title is supported by historical and cultural examples taken from our oral and written literature, in most cases directly from primary sources that recorded how Hawaiians acted, reacted, responded, and behaved in different situations. Our goal is to make this knowledge more accessible to teachers, parents, and students.

Knowing how our ancestors behaved begs the question of whether we are doing the same. If we are practicing our culture in a way similar to how they did, then we know that Hawaiian culture is very much alive today. If we do things differently, we have to ask if those changes have been to our benefit, and whether we can reclaim what has been forgotten, lost, or suppressed.

Hoʻoponopono

"We forgave and were forgiven, thrashing out
every grudge, peeve or sentiment among us.
In this way, we became a very closely bound family unit."
- Mary Kawena Pukui

Hawaiʻi historian Samuel Manaiakalani Kamakau described what families in pre-contact and pre-Christian Hawaiʻi did to seek reconciliation and forgiveness.

> The Hawaiians are said to be a people consecrated to the gods; the ʻaumakua gods were "born," and from them man was born.

> When trouble came upon a family for doing wrong against an *ʻaumakua* god [...] (t)he cause for this trouble was shown to them by dreams, or visions, or through other signs sent by the god. It was pointed out to them what sacrifices to offer, and what gifts to present, to show their repentance for the wrong committed by the family. They were to go to the *Pohaku o Kane*, their *puʻuhonua*, where they were to make offerings to atone for their wrong doing *(mohai hala)* and to pacify the god *(mohai hoʻoluʻolu)* [...] (1968, 32)

He also observed

> The *Pohaku o Kane*, the Stone of Kane, was a place of refuge, a *puʻuhonua*, for each family from generation to generation. It was not a heiau; it was a single stone monument [. . .] and a *kuahu* altar with ti and other greenery planted about. There the family went to obtain relief. (1968, 32)

When the high chiefs ended the state religious system in 1819, places of refuge such as Pōhaku o Kāne gradually ceased to be used and other forms of seeking reconciliation developed.

Mary Kawena Pukui in a Fritz Henle photograph, reprinted courtesy of the Henle Archive Trust.

Today, a "descendant" of those early forms of reconciliation is still practiced. It survives largely through the efforts and determination of Mary Kawena Pukui, formerly a translator and consultant at the Bernice Pauahi Bishop Museum in Hawai'i.

When interviewed by the museum nearly fifty years ago, Pukui spoke of a way in which Hawaiians were able, on a course to healing, to "set to right first" mental problems. The interview was tape-recorded and transcribed. Pukui called this way of mental cleansing ho'oponopono.

She noted in the interview, "Today, the ho'oponopono remains only a fond memory since the death of my mother in 1942. [. . .] The ho'oponopono is rare today and is regarded as a silly remnant of heathenism by most people and squelched at every turn" (Tape H-41G, 7/10/1958). Pukui was afraid that this way of life would soon be forgotten.

From the mid 1960s through the early 1970s, Pukui had the opportunity to ensure that this part of Hawaiian culture would not die. She collaborated with mental health professionals and social workers at the Queen Lili'uokalani Children's Center to codify the cultural practice in systematic terms that could be understood and learned by modern professionals and families. She wanted to ensure that Hawaiian families would once again be able to use ho'oponopono.

A Hawaiian Way of Healing

What is hoʻoponopono? Why is it so special and important? Pukui described it in these words.

> My people believed that the taking of medicine was of little help without first removing any and all mental obstructions. [. . .] When a problem arose in the family affecting an individual or the group as a whole, every member of the immediate family turned to the hoʻoponopono. [. . .] Every one of us searched our hearts for any hard feelings of one against the other and did some thorough mental house cleaning. We forgave and were forgiven, thrashing out every grudge, peeve or sentiment among us. In this way, we became a very closely bound family unit. (Tape H-41G, 7/10/1958)

According to Pukui, only then would the afflicted family members be ready to be healed. The burden of the problems needed to be lifted from their minds before their bodies were ready for medical treatment.

The word hoʻoponopono itself hints at such a process. The root of the word is "pono" which has a multitude of meanings. The scholar Davida Malo indicated that pono was the absolute model of good behavior and values in traditional Hawaiian society. All persons, including chiefs, strived to be pono.

> There were also many thoughts considered to be pono maoli [*truly pono*], but misfortune could quickly come about. It was pono when one's eyes saw something and one's heart desired it, but one was hoʻomanawanui [*patient*] and did not go to take it, but quickly left forgetting about it without even touching it. This was pono.

Furthermore, it was not considered correct behavior to grab things, to lie, to flock into a person's doorway, to look longingly at something, or to beg for someone's things. This was pono.

There were several other things considered to be pono: being well supplied, not being shiftless, not exposing oneself to others, not being irresponsible, and not eating someone else's food. This was pono.

Furthermore it was pono for a husband and wife to live together, to have children, friends [. . .]

These things were considered pono: not to over indulge in pleasure and fun [. . .]

These were things a person could do to greatly improve (pono) the quality of life (ka noho 'ana ma keia ola 'ana). Great was the pono of these things. (187–88)

When a word in Hawaiian is repeated, it is done to give emphasis and underscore its importance. The prefix, ho'o, is a causative, that is "to do something" or "to make something happen." Hence, the term ho'oponopono is "to make very pono."

A year before being interviewed, Pukui had worked on the publication of a modern Hawaiian-English dictionary. In this 1957 publication, ho'oponopono is described as "Mental cleansing: the old Hawaiian method of clearing the mind of a sick person by family discussion, examination, and prayer" (314).

Following Pukui's work on the publication *Nānā I Ke Kumu* with the Culture Committee at Queen Lili'uokalani Children's Center, the 1986 revised *Hawaiian Dictionary* described ho'oponopono as "Mental cleansing: family conferences in which relationships were set right through prayer, discussion, confession, repentance, and mutual restitution and forgiveness [. . .]" (341).

Pukui pointed out that hoʻoponopono is directly related to healing and good health. An understanding of traditional wellness and healing is critical to give clarity to this cultural concept and the process of hoʻoponopono.

We know that traditional Hawaiian ideas about being sick are complex. In Hawaiian terms, being ill is more than being injured or affected by a physical ailment or disease. People believed that sickness could be inflicted by spirits or by the breaking of a kapu. These types of sicknesses were made known through painful physical and mental forms or even through conflicts between individuals, families, and groups.

The treatment, or healing, of these types of sicknesses is very complicated and requires great skill and flexibility. Diagnosis involves the consultation of the healer with the sick person, his or her family, and even the extended family or community. In many situations the healer is also a relative of the ill person.

A traditional healer uses his or her skills in observation and dialogue to gain an understanding of the family's or group's insights in order to determine the degree and type of sickness and the approaches to be used for healing. Without such a collaborative diagnosis, it would be extremely difficult to pinpoint the type of illness and to allay any doubts or fears on the part of the ill person. These consultative diagnoses serve to improve the chances of healing. This approach is not only holistic, it also targets the root causes for "sickness" instead of just its symptoms or manifestations, such as being tired or having a cold.

> [The] key element to this process is the often and lengthy consultations with the patient, his or her family and extended family, where a ʻsick person is not treated as an isolate, but rather (he or she) is considered in the context

of family relationships.' It is during these sessions that people are encouraged to air any grievances which might be causing tension within the family, problems concerning illnesses, and other difficulties encountered so that the appropriate treatment may be revealed. (Chun 2)

The airing out of patient's and the family's mistakes and transgression mirrors what a student learning to be a traditional healer must do. He or she must forgive him or herself of previous wrongs before entering into the priesthood to the forgiveness (reconciliation) of others. But we find that it was the kahuna 'anā'anā kuni, a class of priest not usually thought of today as being associated with healing, who were responsible to forgive (kalahala) the trespasses of other people. Kamakau points out that kalahala, a term that Hawaiian Christianity associates with "forgiveness" was "one of his duties."

> [. . .] One of his duties as a *kahuna 'ana'ana* in his practice of *kuni* (*iloko o kana 'oihana kuni*) was to *kalahala*—remove the grounds for offense within the victim, and so remove (*wehe*) the affliction (*make*) sent by another. (1968, 122)

This lesser known aspect of traditional healing practices is corroborated by Kamakau's contemporary Zephyrin Kahoāli'i Kepelino in a brief article entitled "Te Tala." Although the translators rendered it as "counter-sorcery," te tala literally means "to forgive," and inserting it into the translation gives us support to Kamakau's statement.

> Forgiveness (te Tala) is something associated with all the priests involved with sorcery. The skilled guardian of sorcery was able to counter (te tana 'ana) the sorcery of other. This was the true priest and one who was not able to do so was unskilled (holona).

> There were two important things in sorcery: causing death
> ('o te tala mate) and restoring health ('o te tala ola). [. . .]
> This is what is first done: he first examines (ho'otolotolo)
> himself, to see what errors and deeds he has done wrong
> against the person who wants to harm him. (Kirtley &
> Mo'okini 58)

The implication of this information is the development of
ho'oponopono, as a family practice, from a merger of two forms
of traditional healing, possibly after their practice decreased, due
to modernization and the spread of Christianity.

The radical changes to Hawaiian society and culture that may
have led to the development and evolution of ho'oponopono,
have also led to its near demise. The findings of the Culture
Committee at Queen Lili'uokalani Children's Center indicated
that common understandings of ho'oponopono were greatly
lacking. They noted

> Many Hawaiians came to believe their time honored
> method of family therapy was "a stupid, heathen thing."
> Some practiced *ho'oponopono* secretly. As time went on,
> Hawaiians remembered, not *ho'oponopono* but only bits and
> pieces of it. Or grafted-on innovation. Or mutations. Or
> complete distortions of concept, procedure and vocabulary.
>
> In the past five years, Center staff members have compiled
> an almost unbelievable list of incomplete or distorted
> explanations of what *ho'oponopono* is. Most—but not all—
> come from clients. (Pukui, Haertig, & Lee, 1972, 69)

In order to dispel these mistaken beliefs and to gain a better
knowledge of ho'oponopono, it is important that one understands
historical and traditional Hawaiian roots of the healing and
peacemaking processes.

Traditional Accounts of the Process of Healing and Peacemaking

The process of consulting and counseling was used by the early Hawaiians for healing of the greater community, especially during times of crisis. This form of peacemaking had no particular name, but its similarities to ho'oponopono are remarkable. With a better understanding of the process of ho'oponopono, we are now able to revisit known historical events where the elements can be observed in action. There are several significant occurrences that have been recorded and that provide a powerful image of the effectiveness of this process.

Through interviews with living informants recorded by the historian Samuel Manaiakalani Kamakau, the earliest account recalls a battle between Alapa'i, the paramount chief of Hawai'i, and the chiefs of O'ahu allied with Peleiōhōlani of Kaua'i. The battle was to take place on the beach of Nāoneala'a in Kāne'ohe on the island of O'ahu.

> Now there was a certain wise counselor named Na-'ili, brother to Ka-maka'i-moku the mother of Ka-lani-'opu'u and Keoua, who was the chief in charge of Wai'anae. [. . .] Said Na-'ili to Pele-io-holani, "It would be best for you to put an end to this war and you two become acquainted with Alapa'i," and he continued, "You can stop this war if 0you will, for the chiefs of Maui and Hawaii are related to you and that not distantly, for they are your own cousins." "Is Alapa'i related to me?" asked Pele-io-holani. "You are a god, and on one side you are related," answered Na-'ili. So Pele-io-holani consented to a meeting with Alapa'i.

At the time the fighting was going on at Kaulekola in Kane'ohe, and Na-'ili went down to stop the fighting. Approaching Ka-lani-'opu'u and Keoua, he kissed their hands and asked, "Where is your uncle?" Ka-lani-'opu'u said, "Alapa'i? He is at the seacoast at Waihaukalua." "Then stop the fighting and let us go down to the seacoast." The two consented and went down with Na-'ili to the coast with the chiefs and fighting men of Hawaii, and those of Oahu and Kauai also retired. There Na-'ili met Alapa'i, and the two wailed over each other affectionately. "What brings you here?" said Alapa'i. "I have come to stay the battle while you go to meet Pele-io-holani." "Does he consent?" "Yes," answered Na-'ili. So Alapa'i agreed to stay the battle and go to meet Pele-io-holani. Then Na'ili laid down the terms of the conference. They were to meet at Naoneala'a. The Hawaiian forces were to remain in their canoes; not one was to land on pain of death except Alapa'i himself, and he was to land without weapon in his hand; likewise in the forces of Kauai and Oahu, if even a single chief bore arms, he was to die.

The beach of Nāoneala'a, Kāne'ohe, O'ahu, reprinted courtesy of Norman Shapiro

It was the custom, when blood relatives went to war with each other and both sides suffered reverses, for some expert in genealogies to suggest a conference to end the war; then a meeting of both sides would take place. So it was that Pele-io-holani and Alapa'i met at Naoneala'a in Kane'ohe, Ko'olaupoko, on Ka'elo 13, 1737, corresponding to our January. The two hosts met, splendidly dressed in cloaks of bird feathers and in helmet-shaped coverings beautifully decorated with feathers of birds. Red feather cloaks were seen on all sides. Both chiefs were attired in a way to inspire admiration and awe, and the day was one of rejoicing for the end of a dreadful conflict. [...] Between the two chiefs stood the counselor Na-'ili, who first addressed Pele-io-holani saying, "When you and Alapa'i meet, if he embraces and kisses you let Alapa'i put his arms below yours, lest he gain the victory over you." [...] Alapa'i declared an end of war, with all things as they were before, the chiefs of Maui and Molokai to be at peace with those of Oahu and Kauai, so also those of Hawaii. Thus ended the meeting of Pele-io-holani with Alapa'i. (1992, 71–72)

However, within a year the two sides were at odds again. Kamakau remarked, "It was thought that this was a family quarrel, but it seems to be a real war of rebellion." However, Kamakau noted, "the two ruling chiefs met there again, face to face, to end the war and become friends again, so great had been the slaughter on both sides. [...] Perhaps the reason for this friendliness on the part of the two chiefs was the close relationship that existed between them" (1992, 72).

What can we learn from the above description that helps to identify the process of mending a broken relationship? How does it work?

- ❋ It takes a wise counselor who knows or is familiar with all parties involved [a genealogist] to go beyond blind rivalries and emotions.

- ❋ It takes the willingness and consent of all parties to stop the fighting and agree to meet.

- ❋ A conference is called.

★ Ground rules and the meeting site are established and agreed upon by the participants.

★ All involved are eyewitnesses to the outcomes.

★ The peace returns the situation back to what it was before the conflict began.

Through Kamakau's comments, we learn that the second outbreak of fighting illustrates that such agreements were not always kept, perhaps because there were deeper causes that remained unaddressed. However, once again the process of meeting was used to bring the parties to peace.

The next event illustrates early forms of hoʻoponopono that took place on the island Maui when the chiefs of Hawaiʻi set out to conquer Kahekili, the paramount chief of Maui. It was known as the battle of Kakanilua.

Having established a massive fleet of canoes offshore on the leeward coast of the island, the first wave of eight hundred warriors attacked on the shoreline dressed with feather capes that reflected the colors of the rainbow: red, yellow, and dark green-blue. They moved across the plains and towards the sand dune hills. Their helmets stood out like the crescent moon, but when they reached the sand dunes they were caught in an ambush like fish that had entered the gates of a fishpond. They were immediately surrounded by a fine meshed net made up of the defending Maui warriors. These forces had swarmed behind the sand dunes cutting off the invading force from the rear. They were routed and the dead were piled up like tree branches or fish caught up in a net. It was said that only two of the eight hundred warriors escaped.

While this was occurring, the chief of the invading warriors, Kalani'ōpu'u, remained offshore on a canoe where he boasted and bragged of how his warriors must have reached their goal. He was shocked by the bad news that the two surviving warriors brought to him.

A war council was held with the remaining warriors and war chiefs to prepare for the next day's battle. The second wave of invaders was caught in a trap. It was reported that the spears rained down upon the warriors like thick waves that pound the shoreline at high tide. The dead were picked up like grasshoppers to be burnt in huge piles. It was at that moment Kalani'ōpu'u sought a means to stop the killing.

> When Ka-lani-'opu'u saw that the forces of Hawaii were surrounded by Ka-hekili's men he said to Ka-lola his chiefess, "Oh Hono-ka-wailani! we shall all be killed. Do go up to your brother Ka-hekili to sue for peace." Ka-lola answered, "It will not do any good for me to go, for we came to deal death. If we had come offering love we should have been received with affection. I can do nothing. Our only hope lies in Ka-lani-kau-i-ke-aouli Kiwala'o." "Perhaps Ka-hekili will kill my child," said Ka-lani-'opu'u. "Ka-hekili will not kill him. We will send Ka-hekili's half brothers with him, Ka-me'e-ia-moku and Ka-manawa." So Kiwala'o was dressed in the garments of a chief and attended by Ka-me'e-ia-moku bearing the spittoon and Ka-manawa carrying the kahili. (Kamakau, 1992, 88)

The young boy, who appeared as if he were covered by a rainbow, walked into the midst of the battle field. Warriors on both sides lay down on the ground because Kīwala'ō's rank demanded such respect. Kamakau commented, "The soldiers of Maui wished to ignore the tabu, regretting the cessation of the fighting, but Kīwala'ō continued on to Wailuku." When they reached the

Maui chief Kahekili they saw that he was surrounded not by warriors but by old men and women and children.

> When the twins and Kiwala'o saw the multitude they said, "We imagined that he was in the midst of a school of fish, but it is only red sea moss." When, at the arrival of Kiwala'o, Ka-hekili heard the words, "Here is your child," he turned his face upward [as a sign of a favorable reception]. Ka-hekili lifted himself up so he could see them. Kiwala'o entered and sat on his chest; and they kissed each other and wailed. Afterward the twins crawled forward and kissed the hands of Ka-hekili. Kiwala'o, being tabu, could not be addressed directly. Ka-hekili accordingly asked them, "Why do you bring the Chief here? If you are in trouble you should have come up here yourselves, lest without my knowledge your chief be killed. " The twins answered, "We do not believe that the chief will be killed. It is we who would have been killed had we left the chief at shore. The chief has been sent to ask for life. Grant us our lives. If the chief dies, we two will die with him (*moe-pu'u*), so our royal brother commanded." Ka-hekili replied, "There is no death to be dealt out here. Let live! Let the battle cease!" And he asked, "Where is your sister [referring to Kalola]?" "At the shore, at Kihepuko'a, and it was she who sent us to the chief," answered Ka-manawa. Then Ka-hekili said to his followers, "Take the fish of Kanaha and Mau'oni and the vegetable food of Nawaieha down to Kiheipuko'a." So the two chiefs became reconciled [. . .]" (Kamakau, 1992, 88–89)

Another native historian, John Papa 'Ī'ī, wrote about the same event with a slight difference.

> Kalola, the mother of Kiwalao, was there with her brother Kahekili; and while they were conversing with Oulu a voice proclaiming the *kapu moe*, or prostrating kapu, was heard. "The chief Kiwalao must be approaching," said Kahekili. "Remove my head covering (a wig) quickly." Then Kahekili saw that Keawe a Heulu was in front with the kapu stick

and that behind Kiwalao were Kahekili's younger cousins, Kamanawa and Kameeiamoku, one with a feather cape and kahili, and the other with the spittoon and mat, so he said to his sister, "Wait before you remove my wig, for it is a retainer who comes first. When our 'young one,' Kiwalao, comes up, that will be the proper time to remove it."

[...] Then Kiwalao met Kahekili, and an order was given to stop the fighting." (11)

Once again, there are key characteristics present that should be noted:

- Someone is looked to as a bridge or mediator with the other side.

- Knowledge of relationships, status, rank, symbols, and a person's behavior and mannerisms are extremely important tools.

- Knowing what to say and how to say it are critical for mutual understanding.

- The bonds of relationship are primary.

- Generosity is a key outcome when relationships are mended.

'Ī'ī also describes an interesting familial event that occurred when Kamehameha was a young man. Today the basis for this family quarrel may seem archaic and incongruous with modern morals and values, but in the context of Hawaiian traditional culture, it reveals a deep understanding of Hawaiian thought and behavior.

They were the handsomest men of those days, and the chiefesses gave them many gifts. Thus beautiful physiques

and handsome features earned them a livelihood. This led
to trouble with their uncle Kalaniopuu, for they were taken
by Kaneikapolei, wife of Kalaniopuu. This happened twice,
the first time with Kalaimamahu and the second time with
Kamehameha. It was probably in this way that Kaoleioku
was conceived. Their uncle was "peeved" and would not
allow his nephews to see his face. Keawemauhili, who
stepped in as mediator, told his half brother Kalaniopuu to
stop resenting his nephews because everyone knew that a
woman was like an easily opened calabash, or a container
with a removable lid. Upon these words, Kalaniopuu's
anger ceased, and he sent for his nephews to come and see
him. (7)

There are a few elements of note in this event:

* The intervention of a relative as a mediator when some
  obvious problem has caused a disruption in family life is
  useful.

* Well chosen words are used to cause a reconsideration of
  the problem.

* There is an immediate end to hostility and a call to gather
  to restore or mend the broken relationship.

The following event occurred during the reign of Kamehameha
III when he was still a youth and under the guardianship of
his cousins and relatives. As a sacred chief and king, his older
relatives sought influence over him to further their own personal
and political ambitions. The resulting conflict first took place in
'Ewa on the island of O'ahu and quickly spread to the township
and port of Honolulu. An attempt was made to hold a council in
which the two sides could air their differences.

A few days later a council of chiefs was held at the stone house at Pohukaina where were gathered chiefs, commoners, and foreigners to discuss financial matters. Three chiefesses spoke for the chiefs, Ke-ahi-kuni Ke-kau-'onohi, Ka-ho'ano-ku Kina'u, Kuini Liliha. Ke-kau-'onohi opened with the words which appear so often in newspapers today and which I then heard for the first time—"Hawaii of Keawe, Maui of Kama-lala-walu, Oahu of Kakuhihewa, Kauai of Manokalanipo." She spoke of the goodness of God, of guarding what was good and forsaking what was evil, of not worshipping other gods; Jehovah alone was the one true God. Kina'u spoke in the same way. Then Liliha spoke to the people: "Chiefs and people of my chief, hear me. The stink of my name and that of my husband Boki has spread from Hawaii to Kauai. It is said that we do evil and that we have led the young king to do evil, and so he has been taken away to do evil, and so he has been taken away from me. But we are not guilty; it is the white people and the naval officers who are guilty; it is they who tempted the king, and the blame has been put upon me. But I admit I have done wrong." At these words both natives and foreigners shed tears. Then Ka-heihei-maile, who had been sitting on the stairway during the council, rose and spoke about the goodness of God and urged the people to listen to the words of Ka-'ahu-manu and Kau-i-ke-aouli and of Nahi-'ena'ena. Then she added, drawing a figure from the communal method of fishing for sword fish, "In the time of Kamehameha the fisherman swam together in a row, and if one got out of line or lagged behind he was struck by the sharp nose of the fish. So those who do not follow God's word and do not obey our king, but fall out of line, they shall be struck by the sharp sword of the law, so do not lag behind lest you be hurt." As these words fell upon the ears of the people, they applied them to Liliha and raised an uproar and talked of war against Ka-'ahu-manu and the chiefs. When the chiefesses had gone back to Maui, preparations were actually made for the war which was called the Pahikaua [. . .]" (Kamakau, 1992, 300–301)

What more can we discover about the tools and methods of this process?

* Be careful, that is, be full of care, in choosing one's words and how one says them.

* Listen attentively to what others have to say and be extremely careful to hear what another shares.

* Genuine words of regret, "confession," or "guilt" are received with understanding and love.

* Dropping one's personal agenda or wants can bring everyone back together.

* This process can easily fail if everyone is not totally committed to a successful outcome.

There are several common elements or tools described in the above events and the manner in which people used these to resolve the conflicts.

> One of the most important, yet least obvious, skills is to recognize that something is wrong; that is, a person or persons are upset or hurt and are in need of healing. This recognition is based upon having a common understanding and knowledge of the other person(s) and good intuition. The need becomes recognizable because the relationship between persons is strained and not the same as it was previously. What is desired is the return to that previous positive relationship.

> * There is a proverb that says, "In the word there is life and in the word there is death." In a cultural context, it

stresses how important it is that one's word is "good," or what is said is meant. Thus one needs to be very careful of what one says and how one says it. Many times that means having some knowledge about the person or people gathered. One has to think and reflect about the best way in which to say what one wants people to hear.

● Listening is crucial to the process. Listening is not an easy task, especially if one does not agree with what is being said, or does not understand and wants to ask a question. Listening means paying attention to what the other person is saying, and waiting until that person is finished speaking before asking questions or thinking about a response.

● It is important to review, understand, and accept the things that are common and shared between everyone gathered, and to recognize how important it is to maintain positive relationships.

● As much as the above are important tools, they must be guided by a deep emotional understanding based on trust, sincerity, and honesty. Without these guiding principles no amount of discussion and listening will ever lead to any understanding or healing. It will all be hidden by miscommunication and lies, adding to the causes of the trouble.

● A useful way of disarming the quarreling parties is by getting away from the scene of the problem and using a third party to avoid direct conflict; provide leadership, guidance and direction; and allow each side to say all that they have to say and to listen to all that is said.

🌸 It is important to establish the appropriate ground rules to ensure that there is a feeling of trust, safety, and care.

🌸 All those involved must commit to the process, agree to the ground rules, and want an outcome that would restore the broken relationships and provide healing.

However, it must be understood that this process was not, and is not, used for the resolution of violence and abusive behavior. In traditional times during the kingdom, and still today, acts such as murder, abuse, robbery, and other violent crimes were handled by the chiefs, and later, the courts under the law. The Reverend William Ellis reported during his brief stay in the islands that

> In cases of assault or murder, except when committed by their own chief, the family and friends of the injured party are, by common consent, justified in retaliating. When they are too weak to attack the offender, they seek the aid of their neighbours, appeal to the chief of the district, or the king [...]" (306)

Ho'oponopono could be used thereafter as a process for the transition to incarceration or to address the victims and families. Again, we return to the primary purpose of ho'oponopono which is about restoring relationships; it is not about who is right or who is wrong.

The Process of Setting Things to Right

Hoʻoponopono as a process for setting things to right, largely credited to Mary Kawena Pukui, is not a modern day concept. The historical overview demonstrates that the cultural practice was being used during pre- and post-contact periods. This practice appears to have been continuously used and refined by Hawaiians in family, community, and religious (now mostly Christian) life.

In the historical overview, we have seen the use of a mediator to work with conflicting parties, particularly in the second account of the Pahikaua War. The story illustrated how the words of each person, spoken without thought, led to the outburst of emotions that became the root of the problem. When these accounts are compared with the description of hoʻoponopono as practiced by the ʻohana (family) of Mary Kawena Pukui in Kaʻū on the island of Hawaiʻi, we can see how certain related practices and processes emerged. There is even evidence of retaining the pre-missionary period practices of including the ʻaumakua, as seen in the accounts of the Pōhaku a Kāne.

> When a problem arose in the family affecting an individual or the group as a whole, every member of the immediate family turned to the hoʻoponopono. The problem might be lack of employment, physical illness, ill luck or whatever. If it was an illness, the ailing person was asked whether he had a feeling of resentment against anyone, or had committed a deed that he should not have. If he had, he confessed and explained. Then he was asked whether he was convinced

that it was wrong and, if he did, a prayer was offered asking forgiveness of God or gods. The person against whom the feeling of resentment was directed was asked to forgive him, also. If he, in turn, bore an ill will and had thought or spoken evil against him, he must ask to be pardoned. First the patient confessed and was forgiven, then he in turn forgave the trespasses of the others against him. A mutual feeling of affection and willingness to cooperate had to exist in the family and the household before anything further could be done. So it was between the family and the ʻaumakua, all obstructions had to be removed. The current of affection and cooperation had to flow freely between the ʻaumakua and the family also.

The process of hoʻoponopono sometimes took from one to several hours depending on the natures of the individual, whether quick to anger and to curse, or the reverse.

If the process would be lengthy it would be broken up in shorter sessions with periods of rest between so as not to exhaust the patient. [. . .] One did a lot of self-examining during a hoʻoponopono whether one was the patient or not. (Pukui, 1958)

The codification, that is, the detailed description and explanation, of this process with the publication of *Nānā I Ke Kumu* in 1972, led to wider recognition and use of hoʻoponāopono. Its revival from that time until the present has seen an evolution of the process towards a social work, group therapy, or psychological orientation and away from what appears to be its original intent as a step in the process of traditional healing. This shift away from its historical roots was reinforced with state legislation in 1965 that prohibited the practice of Native Hawaiian healing and contributed to the demise of the knowledge and skills of traditional healing.

Current practice has seen the role of mediator, facilitator, or haku fall upon religious leaders and trained professionals such as social workers and lawyers. More recently, a wide range of interested persons have attended training workshops or classes on ho'oponopono. Pukui noted that "most ho'oponopono did not go beyond the door of our house [. . .] (b)ut with some [other families] a kahuna from outside handled the ho'oponopono" (Tape 41-G, 7/10/1958). Recently, there have even been suggestions that practitioners of ho'oponopono should be licensed as are other health-related professionals, although this would be contrary to Pukui's desire that ho'oponopono be retained as a cultural family practice rather than as a professional activity.

In her interview, Pukui spoke of certain terms being used that described "periods of time" during the process. These included "ku i ka mihi, or repentances; ku i ka pule, [which] set a special period of time for prayers; kukulu kumuhana, or present the problem to God; and ho'omalu, (a sheltering) with no loud boisterous talking, arguments, or going to places of pleasure until the kahuna saw fit to lift the probationary periods (Tape 41-G, 7/10/1958).

These terms became descriptive of the stages of the ho'oponopono process as it developed into a "clinical" model. The descriptions of these developmental stages proved to be especially helpful to those unfamiliar with Hawaiian traditional cultural practices. The descriptions of these terms were further defined through the discussions of the Culture Committee at the Queen Lili'uokalani Children's Center and published in 1972 in *Nana I Ke Kumu, Volume I.*

hihia—entangled or entanglement; snarl or snarled; enmeshed (71)

kukulu kumuhana—the pooling of strengths—emotional, psychological, and spiritual, for a shared purpose. Group dynamics characterized by spiritual elements and directed to a positive goal. A unified, unifying force. In broad context, a group, national, or worldwide spiritual force, constructive and helpful in manner. In *ho'oponopono*, the uniting of family members in a spiritual force to help an ill or troubled member.
Secondary meaning—statement of problem and procedures for seeking a solution, as in opening explanation of *ho'oponopono*. (78)

mahiki—to peel off; to pry; as to peel the bark of a tree to judge the wood beneath; to scrape at the skin to remove a tiny insect burrowed beneath the epidermis. Also, to cast out, as of a spirit. (75)

ho'omalu—to shelter, protect, make peace, keep quiet, control, suspend. A period of peace and quiet. Silent period. (77)

mihi—repentance, confession, apology; to repent, confess, apologize. (73)

kala—to release, untie, unbind, let go. (74) (Pukui et al., 1972)

Each term, then, became linked to a stage in the ho'oponopono process. Depending upon the progression and development encountered at each stage, the process could either move on or become circular, being repeated as many times as needed. Some have compared this circular movement to peeling away the layers of an onion, oftentimes leading to another layer upon other layers.

Cordage: A Cultural Analogy

One cultural analogy to the process of ho'oponopono is the making of cordage and the use of that cordage to make an 'upena, or fish net. This is a useful analogy since the terms hihia (entanglement) and kala (to unbind, untie, to forgive or let go) are used in ho'oponopono.

Around the age of seven or eight, I learned how to make fishing nets using cordage, a bamboo shuttle needle, a small rectangle of press board for a gauge, and a nail to hold down the net.

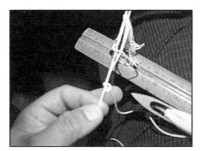
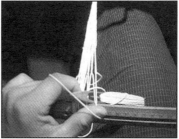

The left photo shows how an individual knot is tied and secured while the right photo shows how a knot is made with several rows completed.

The making of traditional cordage from plant material involves extracting the individual strands of fiber and then rolling and twisting several strands to make up a strong piece of cordage. These collective strands can then be used to make stronger cordage by either twisting them together or actually weaving them. I see the 'ohana in a very similar way: made up from individual fibers but bound together for strength and purpose.

The making of a fish net is a very simple task with the most critical skill being the tying of a tight and secure knot—in fact, several knots—in a straight row. When I first learned this skill, I would often discover after tying down several rows that one or two knots in previous rows were loose. One could go back and try to tighten the knots, but usually that wouldn't work, as it left the triangular holes between knots loose and capable of expanding so that a fish or crab could easily escape.

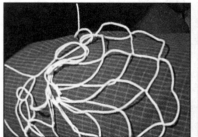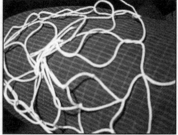

The photo on the left shows tight knots and perfect holes in the beginning stages of a net while the photo on the right shows a mistake where the knot is not tied correctly.

Unfortunately, the solution to this problem was undoing all the knots, working back to the one or two knots that were loose, then re-doing all that work. Making such mistakes taught me some very valuable lessons:

❀ I needed to be very careful about the work that I did, making sure that each knot was tight and secure.

❀ I needed to be patient.

✹ There was no sense in getting angry since mistakes do happen, even if you are being careful.

These lessons also apply to the process of ho'oponopono.

We all make mistakes every day of our lives. How do we go about "untangling" these problems, big or small? Through ho'oponopono we are given a chance to undo both minor and major mistakes by literally going back through events in our lives, back to "knots" that may have been done "wrong," or at least not completed in a desired manner. By correcting those wrongs or mistakes, we can then proceed towards completing our own "net," or life itself.

Contemporary Applications

With the revival of, and growing respect for, traditional Hawaiian cultural practices, interest in utilizing hoʻoponopono in contemporary situations has increased. Several publications and graduate student papers have detailed its practice and demonstrated its application, especially in the mental health field. Family courts have offered hoʻoponopono as a cultural option for Hawaiian families in mediating child custody cases and in marital counseling.

The Boggs and Chun article on hoʻoponopono in the aptly titled "Disentangling" demonstrated that its continued practice suggests the continuing vitality of Hawaiian culture and social structure, contrary to the belief that they had disappeared and were "dead." Shook (101) concluded in her book that "The Hawaiian family certainly deserves to receive the gifts of its own tradition. Furthermore [. . .] [the] potential of hoʻoponopono could expand our understanding of the uses [. . .] and allow for the sharing of this Hawaiian gift."

The recent development of "restorative justice" or "family conferencing" in Aotearoa (New Zealand) appears to fulfill Shook's insight and prediction that, "Further study could also shed light on the understanding of therapeutic universals [. . .] (and) could provide valuable insights into understanding basic principles about assisting people in establishing harmonious interpersonal and social relationships." (102)

Based upon similar traditional practices of the Maori and Samoan communities in New Zealand, the ideas of restorative justice are emerging. Briefly, restorative justice is based on a process that is indigenous, places victims at the center of the justice equation, offers healing to all involved, and lays responsibility for crime in the hands of those who commit it (Consedine 161–164).

Family conferencing has adapted the skills and tools of traditional peacemaking and healing to contemporary life. Family conferencing is increasingly being used in communities throughout the United States and Canada to provide a community and family based option, particularly for non-violent crimes, as a means to ease the burden of the courts.

One account of family conferencing was told by the Reverend Flora Tuhaka of Aotearoa (New Zealand). An incident occurred in a small township on a Saturday when a young Maori teenager vandalized the local bus company. The damage was severe enough that the bus company had to stop its service to the town until the damages were fixed. When the youth was caught, he was headed for criminal charges in court. The bus owner intervened and requested that he would rather have a family conference so that he could speak to the teenager face to face and confront him with the consequences of his actions. At the meeting the owner told of how much disruption was done to the lives of people in the town, some who were the teenager's friends and relatives. The teenager responded that he was sorry, never imagining how much damage he had done by just goofing off because he had nothing better to do during his free time.

Instead of having the offender spend time in a youth facility, the bus owner asked that the youth spend his Saturdays at the company cleaning the place and the buses until he had "paid off" the damages. The idea was that this would provide structure to the teenager's free time, teach him how important the bus service is to the people, and allow him to get to know his own neighbors. The teenager not only did "his time," but after he graduated from school, the bus owner offered the teenager a job at the company because he had performed so well and the owner had gotten to know him.

There is no moral to this true story, but there are some important lessons: many mistakes in life can be corrected, good counsel can be productive in discovering truth, and broken lives and relationships can be mended instead of dismissed and wasted.

Nearly a half century ago, Pukui shared a vision of the re-emergence of ho'oponopono as an important cultural practice to help Hawaiian families heal and strengthen their bonds. Today these very skills and tools have immense educational and social implications if practiced in contemporary life, especially among its youth. Its power and influence lies in the recognition of our basic humanity and the need for healing in every moment of our lives.

Bibliography

Boggs, Stephen T. and Chun, Malcom Nāea. Ho'oponopono: A Hawaiian Method of Solving Interpersonal Problems. In *Disentangling, Conflict Discourse in Pacific Societies*. Ed. Karen Ann Watson-Gegeo and Geoffery M. White. Stanford, CA: Stanford University Press, 1990.

Chun, Malcolm Nāea. OLA: Cultural Perspectives of Hawaiian Health Care. Honolulu: Health Promotion and Education Branch, Hawai'i State Department of Health, 1989.

Consedine, Jim. *Restorative Justice, Healing the Effects of Crime*. Lyttelton, New Zealand: Ploughshares Publications, 1995.

Ellis, William. *Journal of William Ellis*. Honolulu: Advertiser Publishing Co. Ltd., 1963.

Ii, John Papa. *Fragments of Hawaii History*. Bernice P. Bishop Museum Special Publication 70. Trans. Mary Kawena Pukui. Ed. Dorothy B. Barrère. Honolulu: Bishop Museum Press, 1959.

Kamakau, Samuel Manaiakalani. *Ka Po'e Kahiko, The People of Old*. Bernice P. Bishop Museum Special Publication 51. Trans. Mary Kawena Pukui. Ed. Dorothy B. Barrère. Honolulu: Bishop Museum Press, 1968.

Kamakau, Samuel Manaiakalani. *Ruling Chiefs of Hawaii*, (Revised Edition). Honolulu: The Kamehameha Schools Press, 1992.

Kirtley, B. F. & Esther T. Mookini "Kepelino's "Hawaiian Collection": His "Hooiliili Havaii," Pepa I, 1858," in *The Hawaiian Journal of History*, Volume XI, Honolulu: the Hawaiian Historical Society, 1977.

Malo, Davida. *Ka Moolelo Hawaii, Hawaiian Traditions*. Trans. Malcolm Nāea Chun. Honolulu: First People's Productions, 1996.

Pukui, Mary Kawena. *Hooponopono or Setting to Rights*, Tape H-41 G, July 10, 1958. Honolulu: The Bernice Pauahi Bishop Museum.

——, and Samuel H. Elbert, *Hawaiian-English Dictionary*. Honolulu: University of Hawaii Press, 1957.

——, and Samuel H. Elbert, *Hawaiian Dictionary, Revised and enlarged Edition*. Honolulu: University of Hawaii Press, 1986.

——, E. W. Haertig, and Catherine A. Lee. *Nānā I Ke Kumu, Volume I*. Honolulu: Hui Hānai, 1972.

——, E. W. Haertig, and Catherine A. Lee. *Nānā I Ke Kumu, Volume II*. Honolulu: Hui Hānai, 1979.

Shook, E. Victoria. *Hooponopono, Contemporary Uses of a Hawaiian Problem-Solving Process*. Honolulu: University of Hawaii Press, 1985.